History Of Japan For Kids: A History Series

Children Explore Histories Of The World Edition

BABY PROFESSOR
EDUCATION KIDS

Speedy Publishing LLC
40 E. Main St. #1156
Newark, DE 19711
www.speedypublishing.com

Copyright 2018

All Rights reserved. No part of this book may be reproduced or used in any way or form or by any means whether electronic or mechanical, this means that you cannot record or photocopy any material ideas or tips that are provided in this book.

Few nations on Earth have had a more colorful history than Japan. Read and learn more of Japan's rich history!

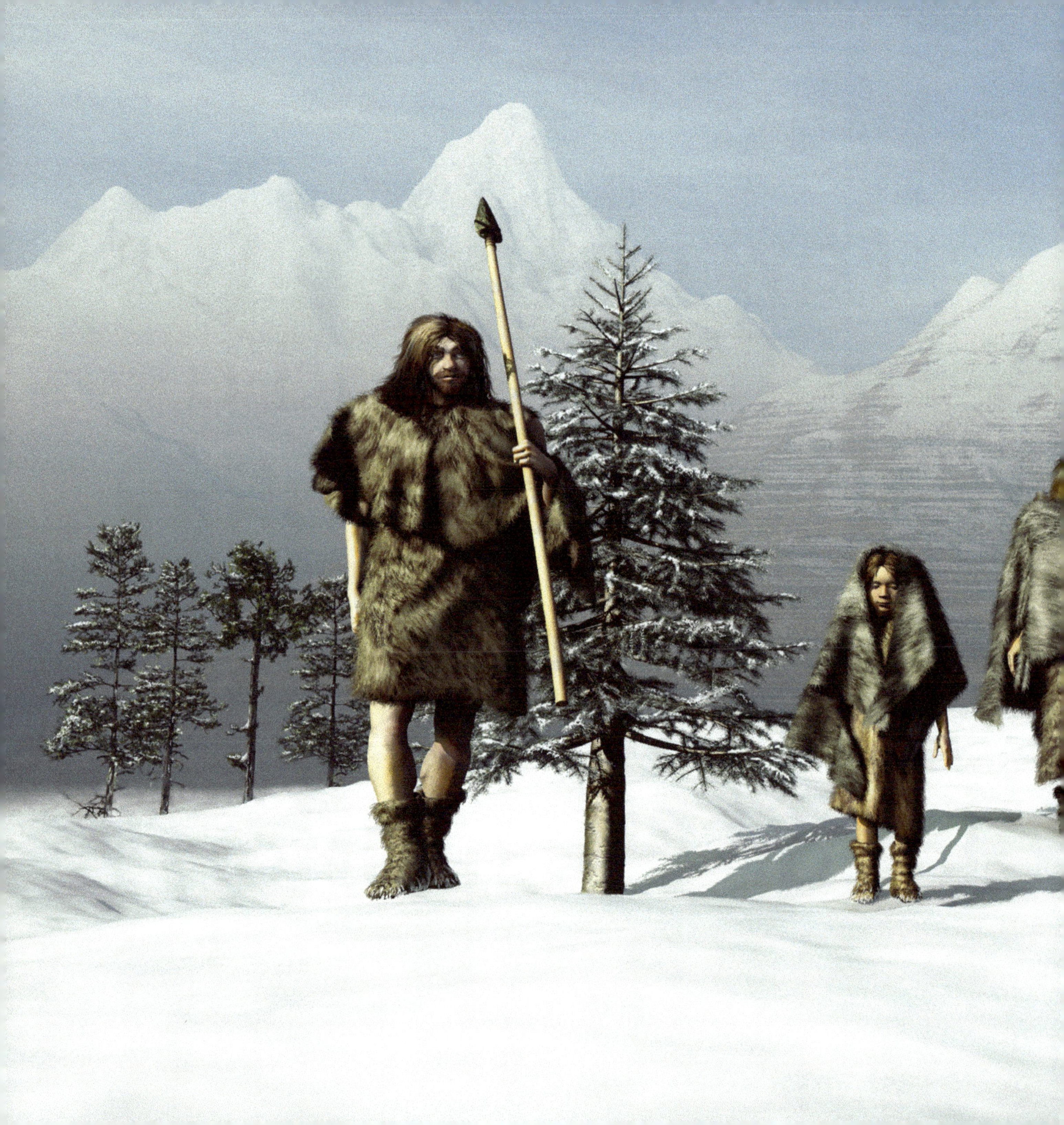

Japan likely was settled about 35,000 years ago by Paleolithic people from the Asian mainland.

At the end of the last Ice Age, about 10,000 years ago, a culture called the Jomon developed. Jomon hunter-gatherers fashioned fur clothing, wooden houses, and elaborate clay vessels.

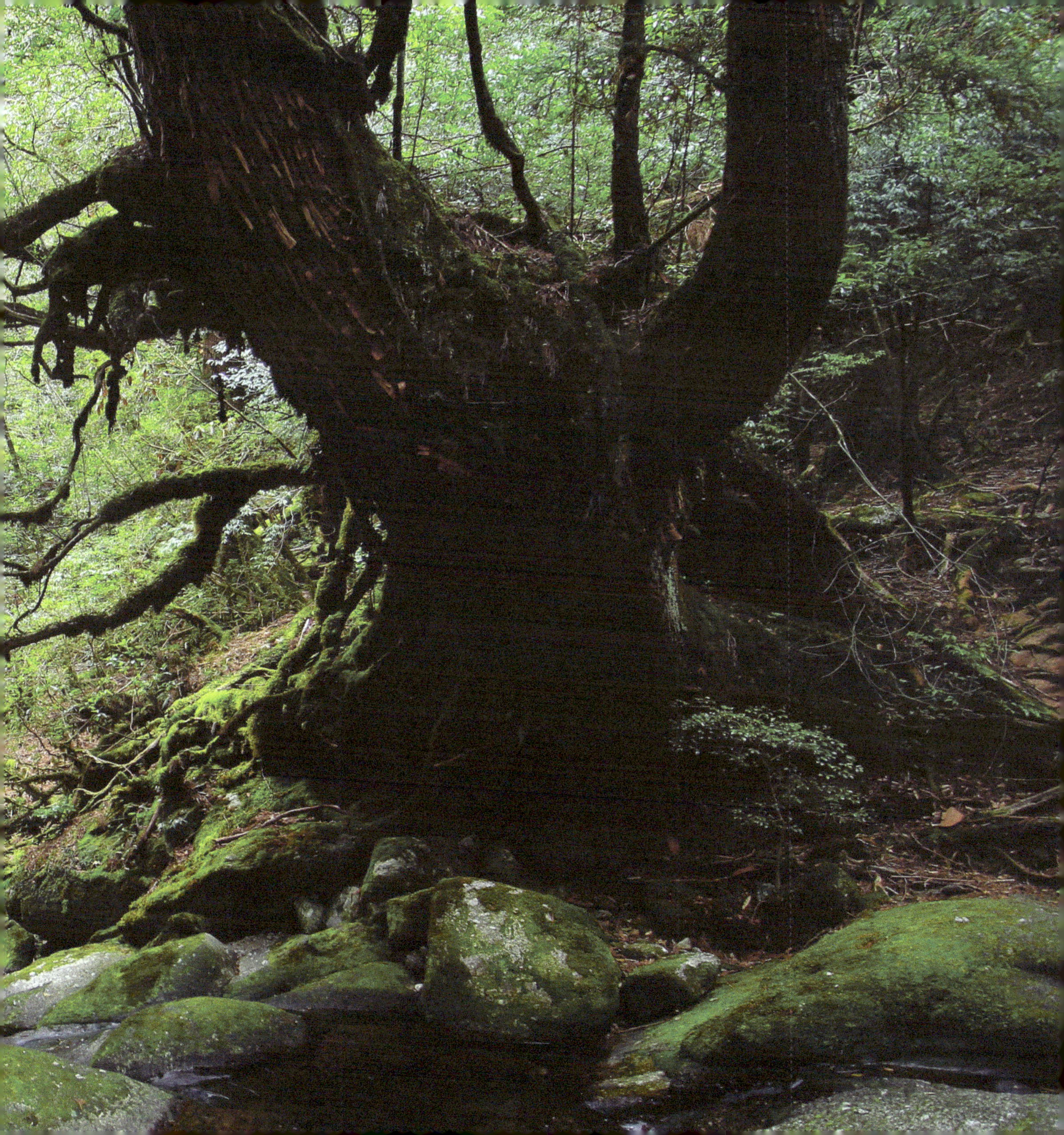

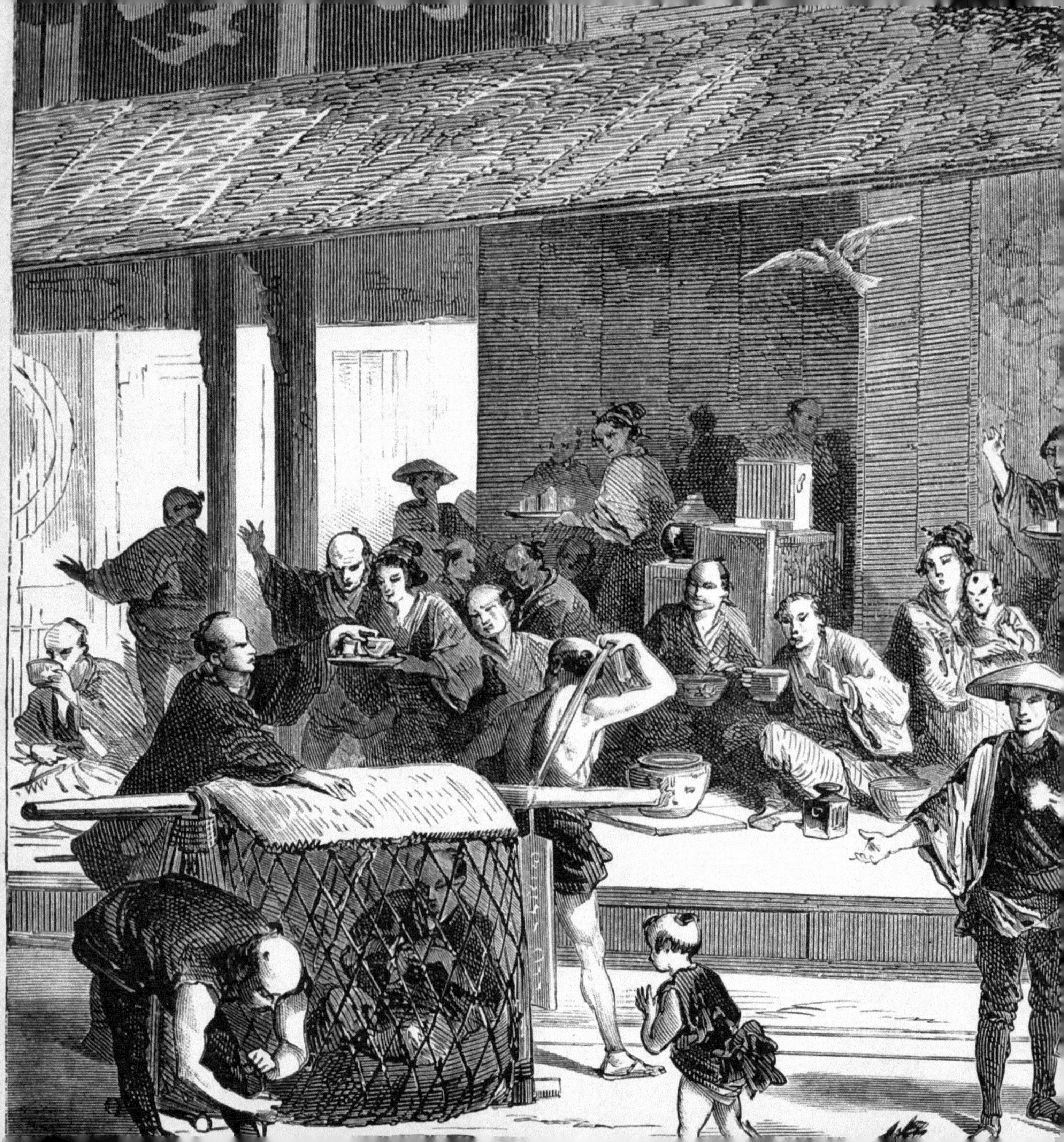

A second wave of settlement around 400 B.C. by the Yayoi people introduced metal-working, rice cultivation, and weaving to Japan.

The first era of recorded history in Japan is the Kofun (250-538 A.D.), characterized by large burial mounds or tumuli.

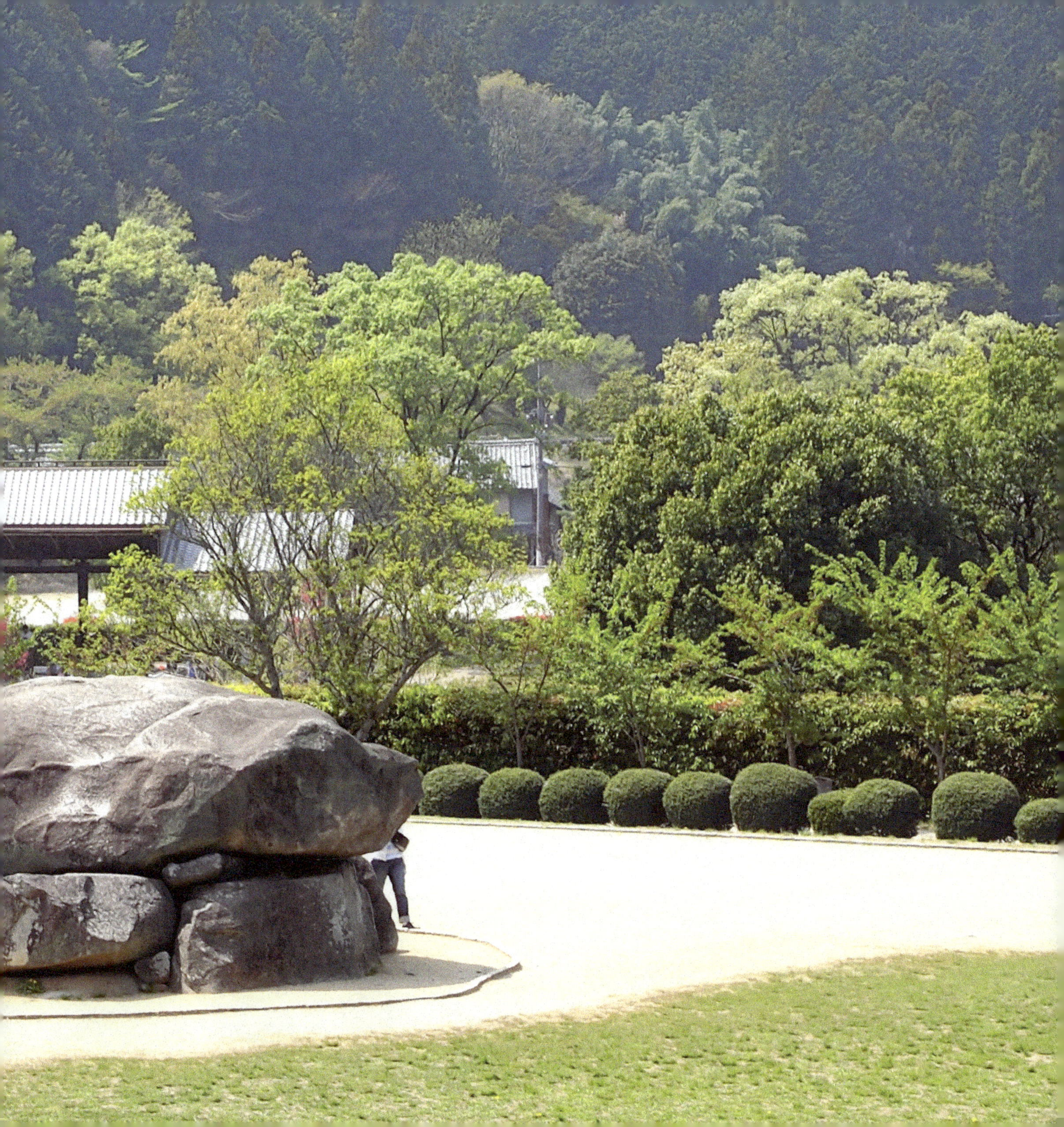

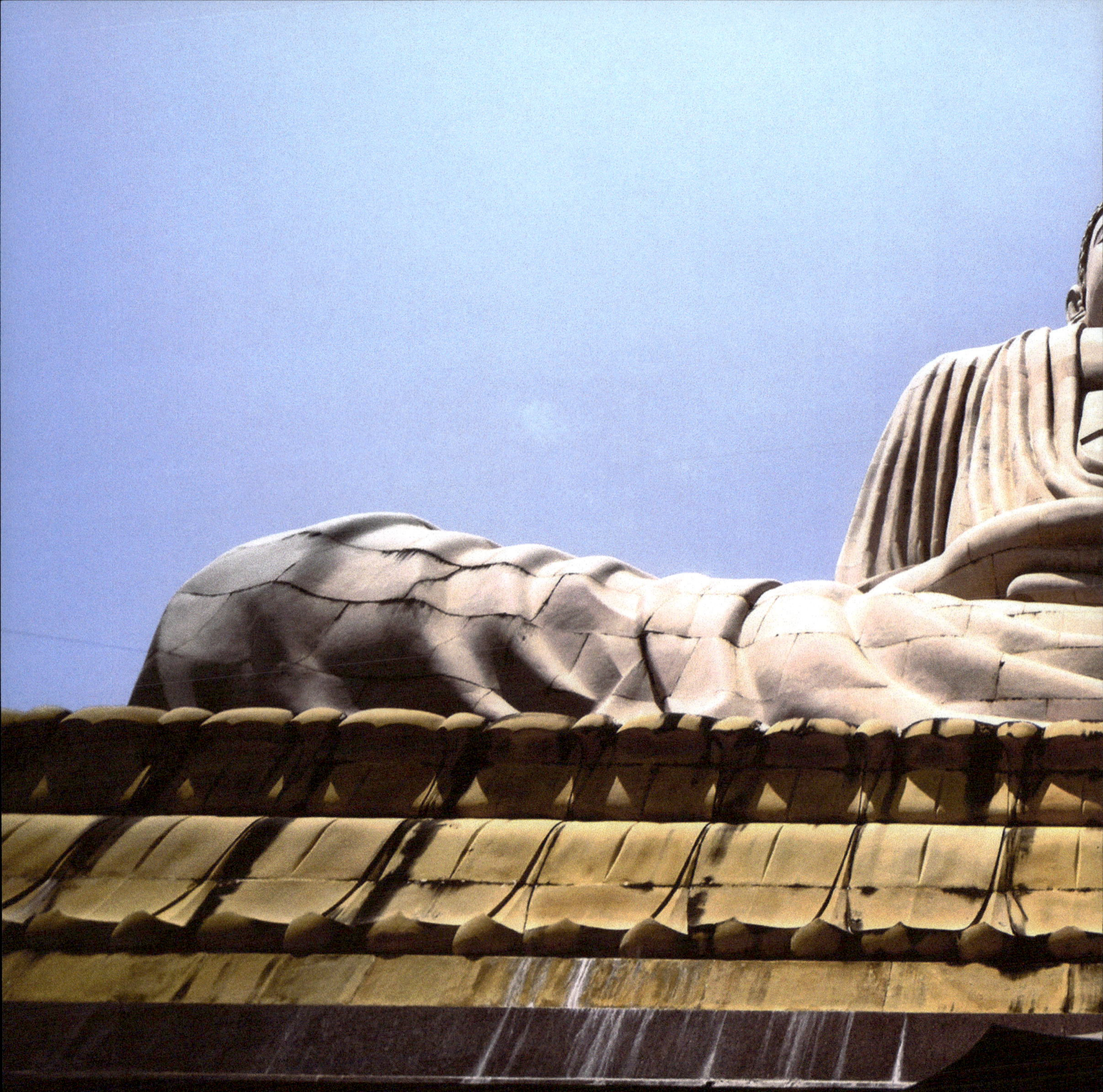

Buddhism came to Japan during the Asuka Period, 538-710, as did the Chinese writing system.

Japan's unique culture developed rapidly in the Heian era, 794-1185, the samurai warrior class developed at this time.

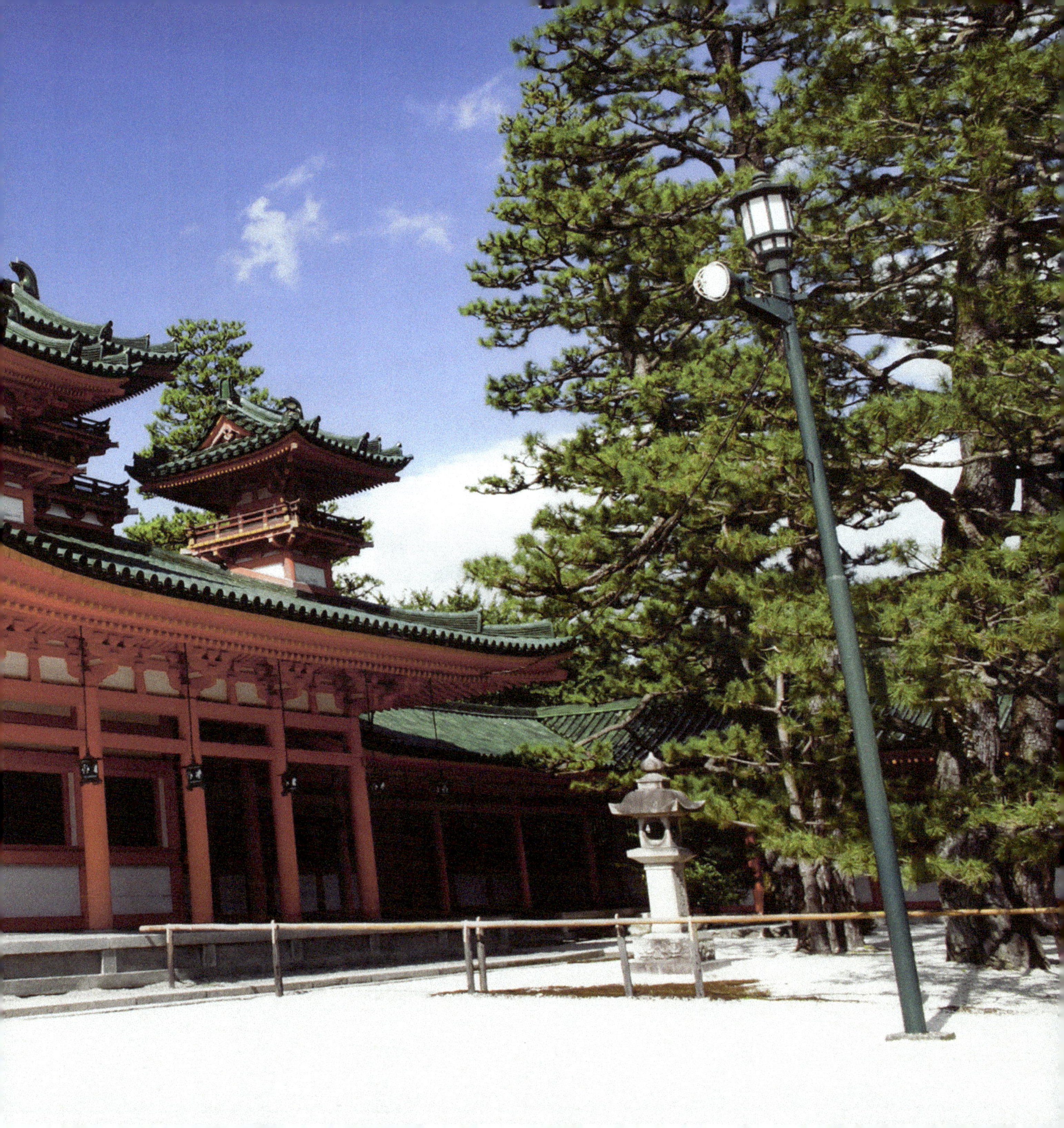

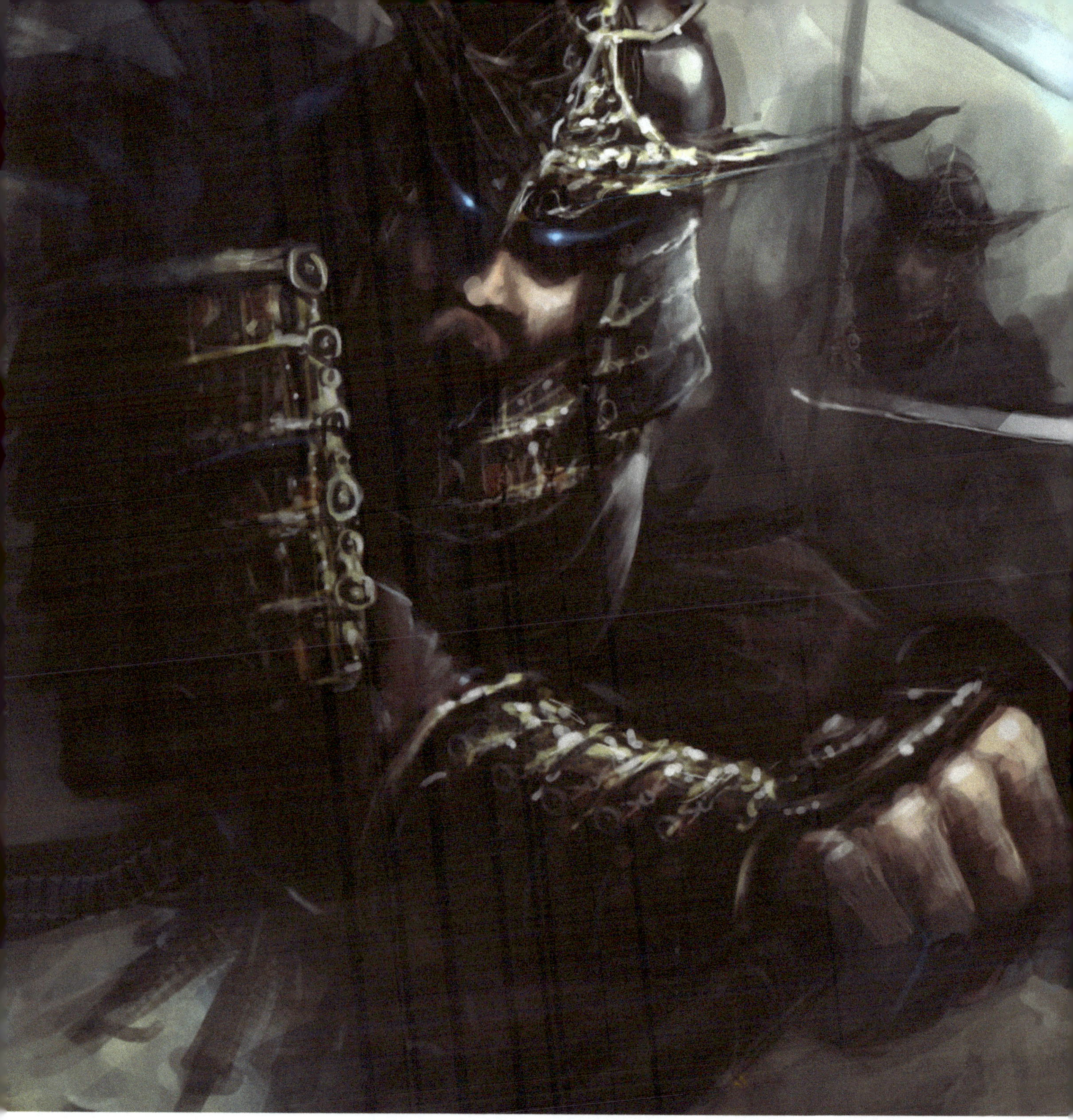

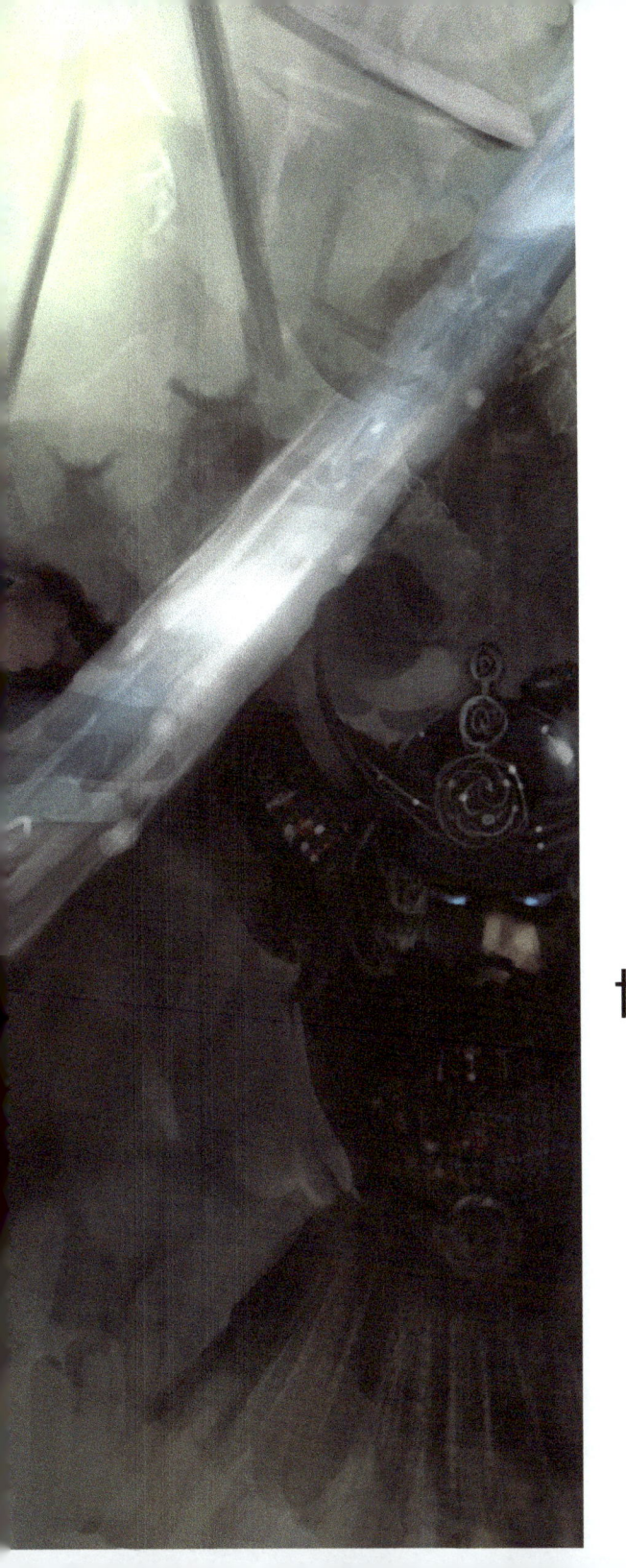

Samurai lords, called "shoguns," took over governmental power in 1185, and ruled Japan in the name of the emperor until 1868.

A strong emperor, Go-Daigo, tried to overthrew shogunal rule in 1331, resulting in a civil war between competing northern and southern courts that finally ended in 1392.

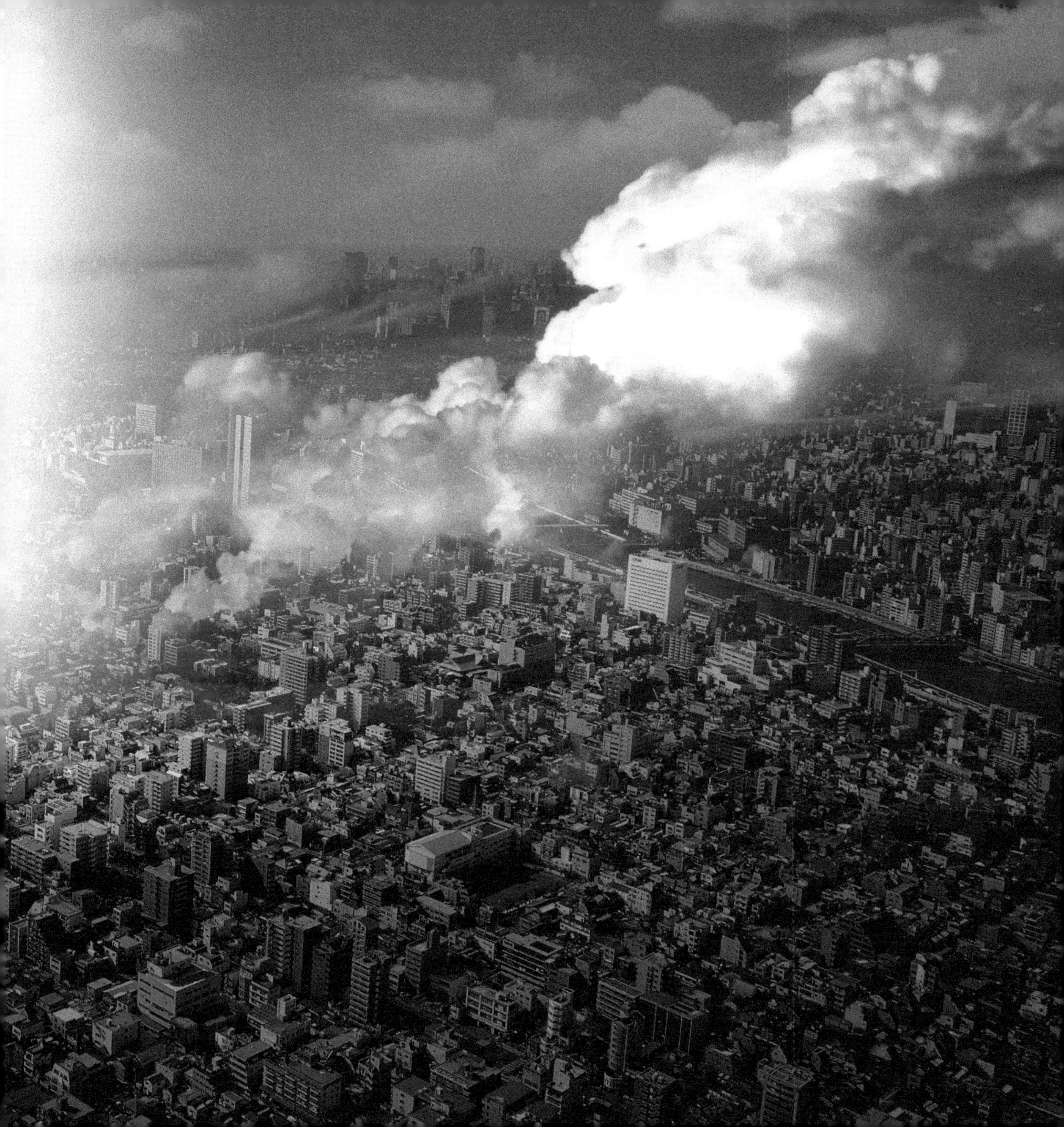

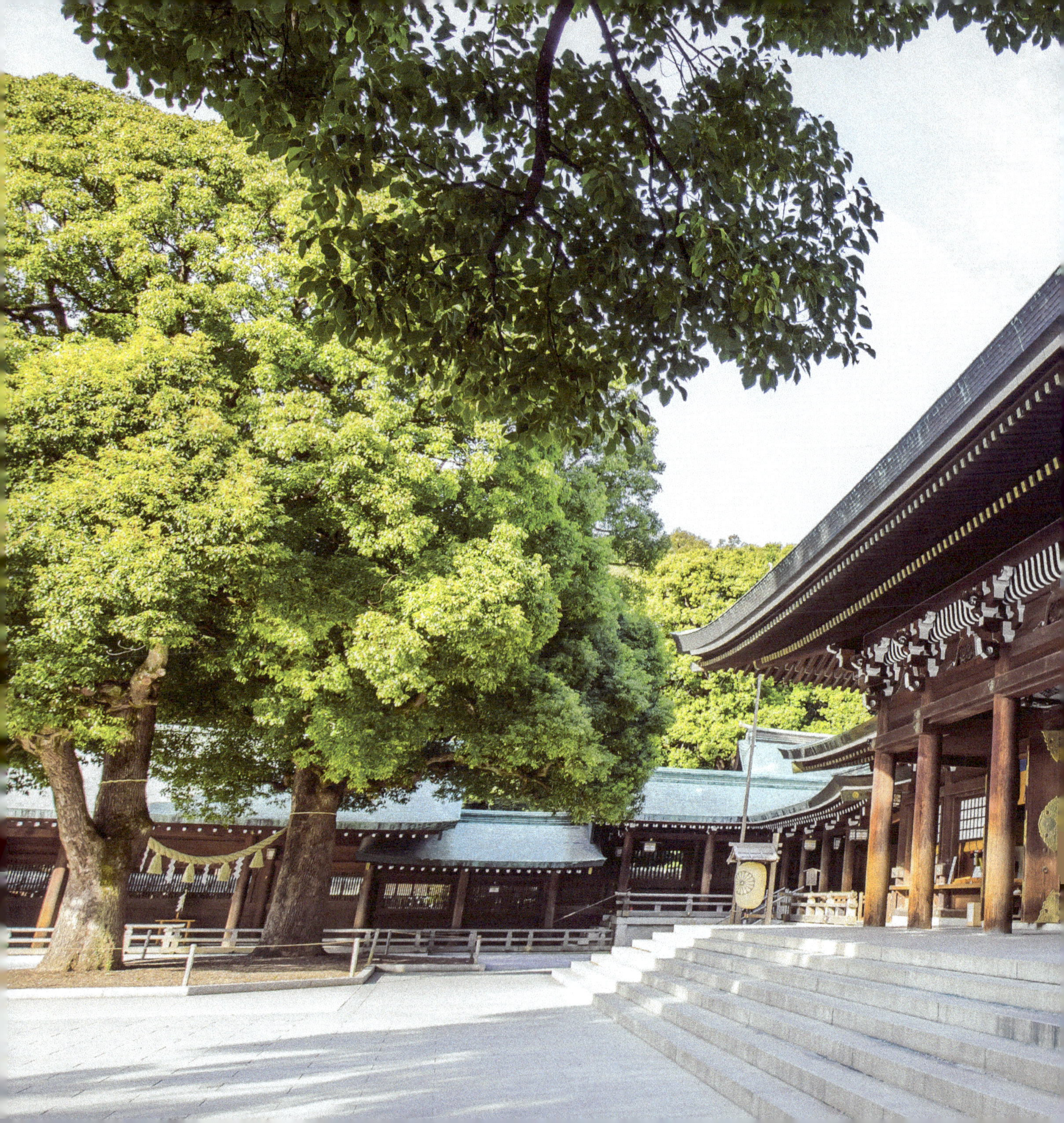

In that year, a new constitutional monarchy was established, headed by the Meiji Emperor. The power of the shoguns was broken.

After the Meiji Emperor's death, his son became the Taisho Emperor (r. 1912-1926).

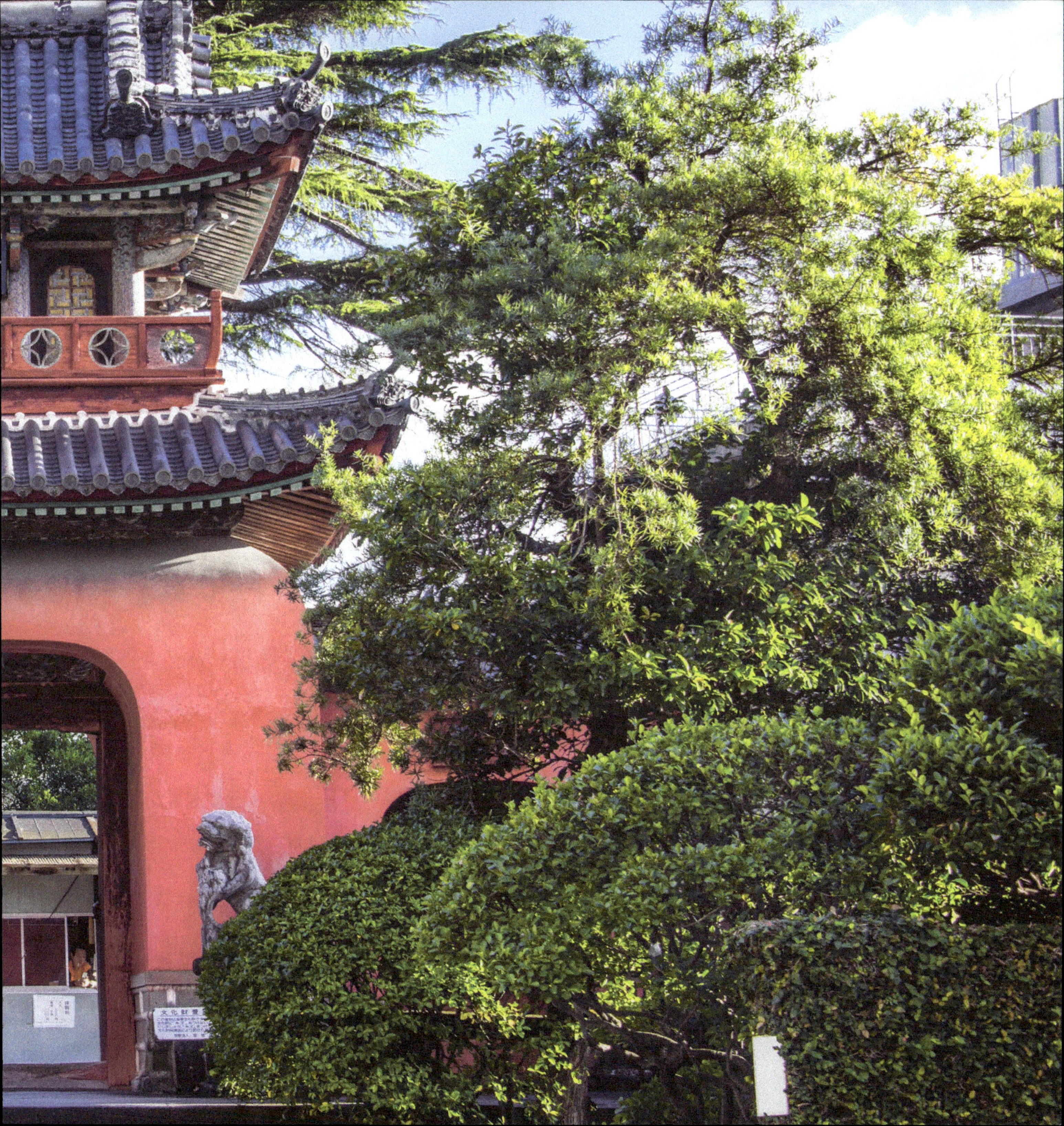

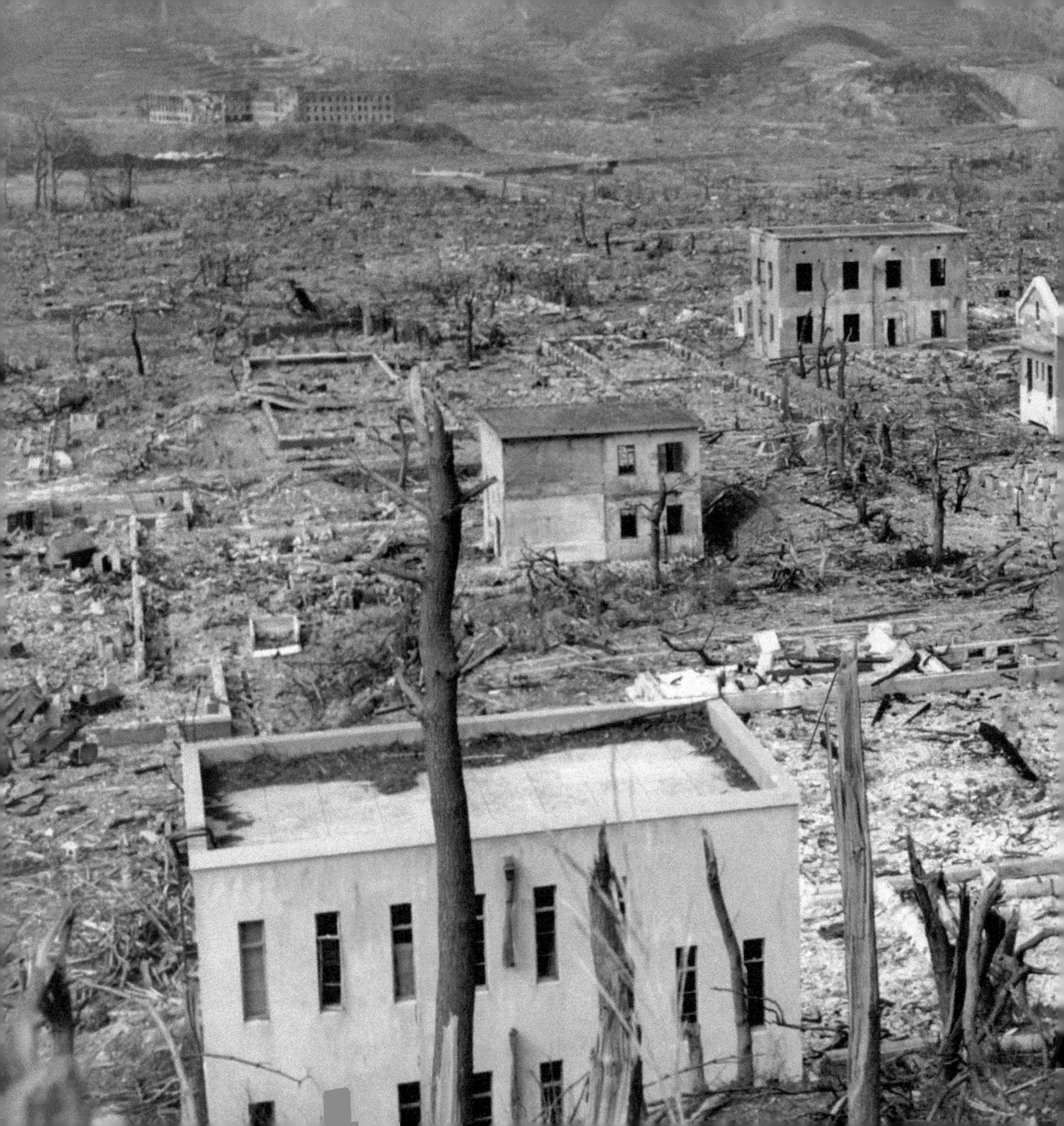

Japan formalized its rule over Korea and seized northern China during World War I.

The Showa Emperor, Hirohito, (r. 1926-1989) oversaw Japan's aggressive expansion during World War II, its surrender, and its rebirth as a modern, industrialized nation.

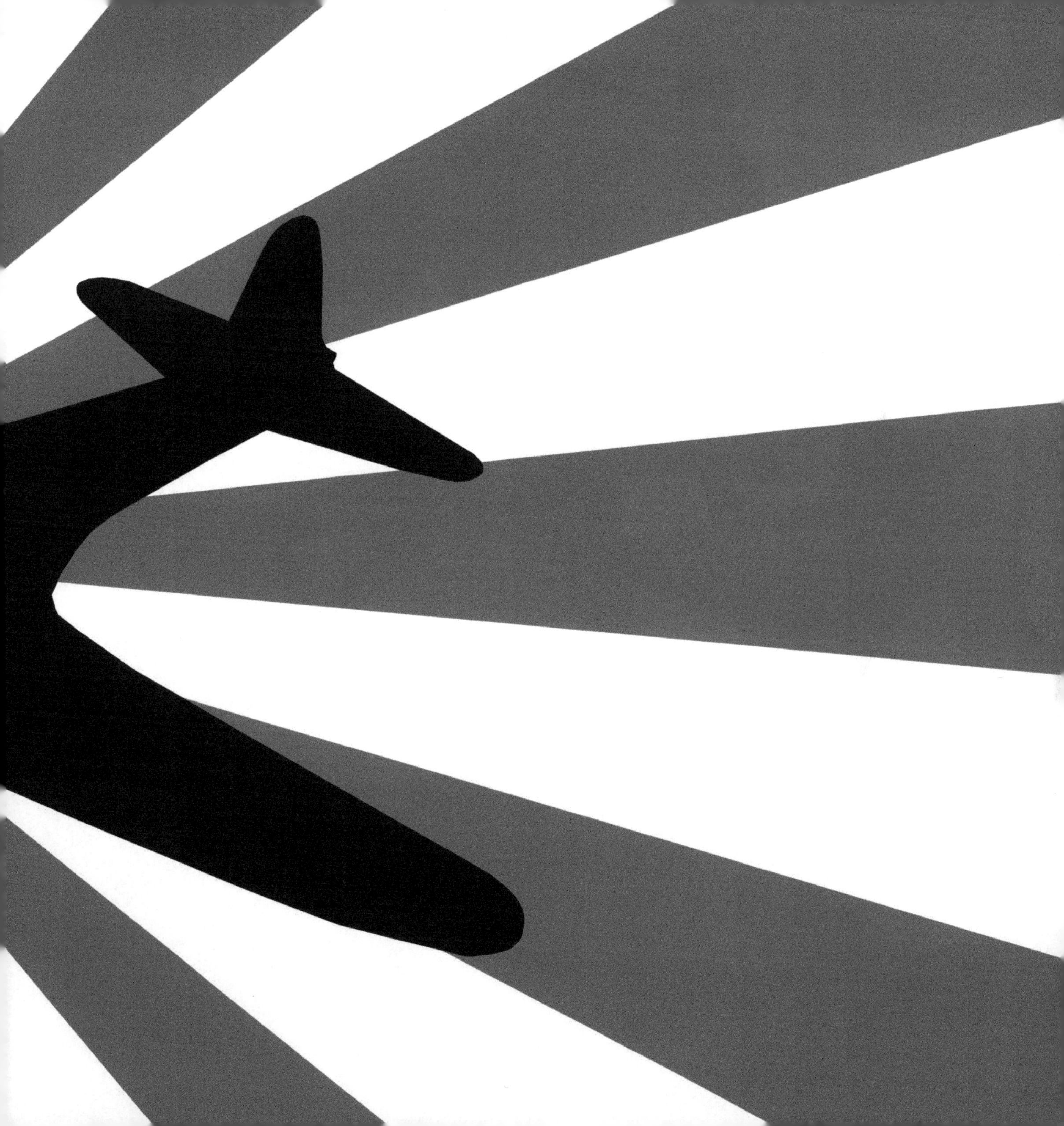

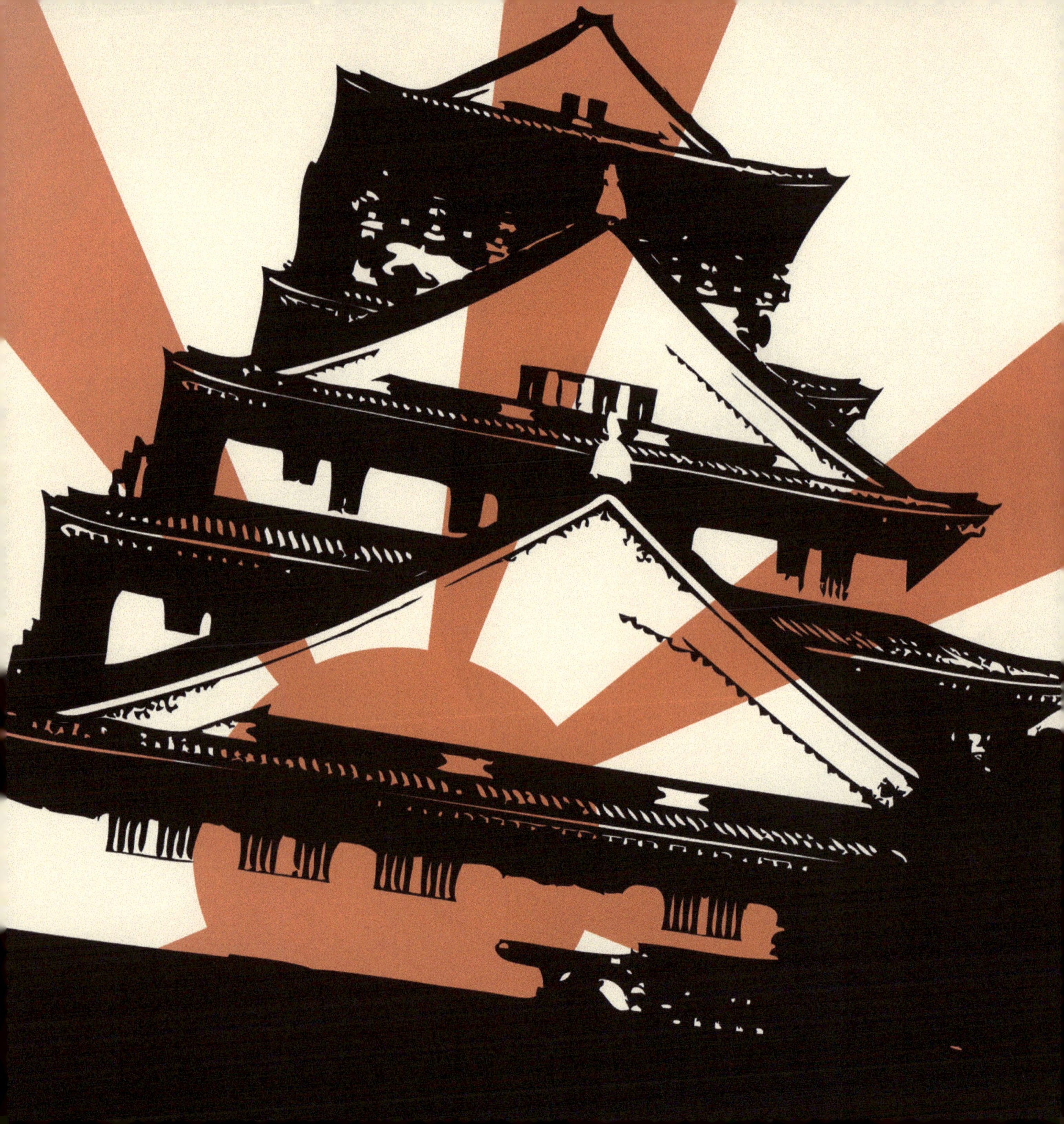

The Four-Tiered Class System of Feudal Japan

The Samurai Class

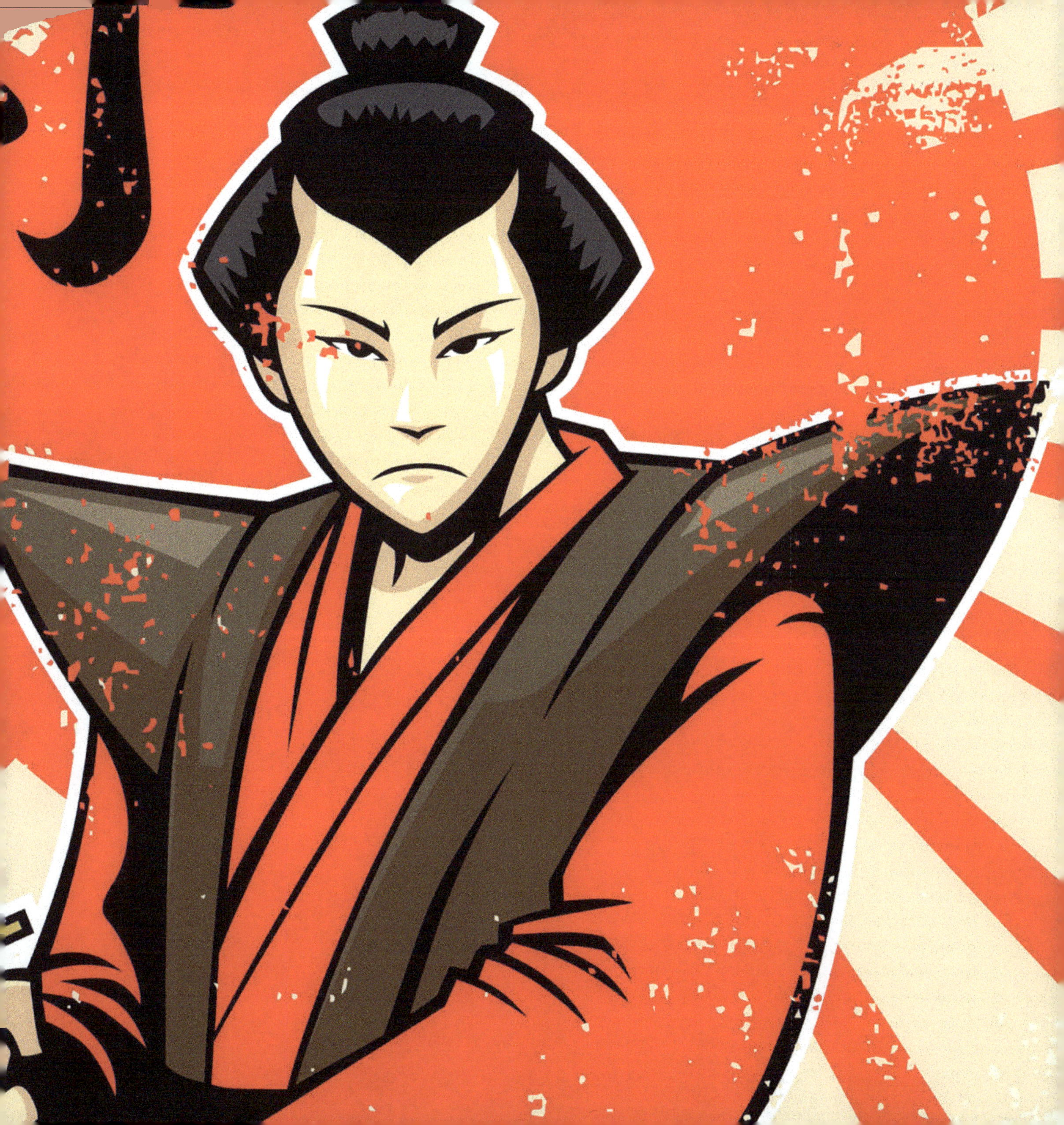

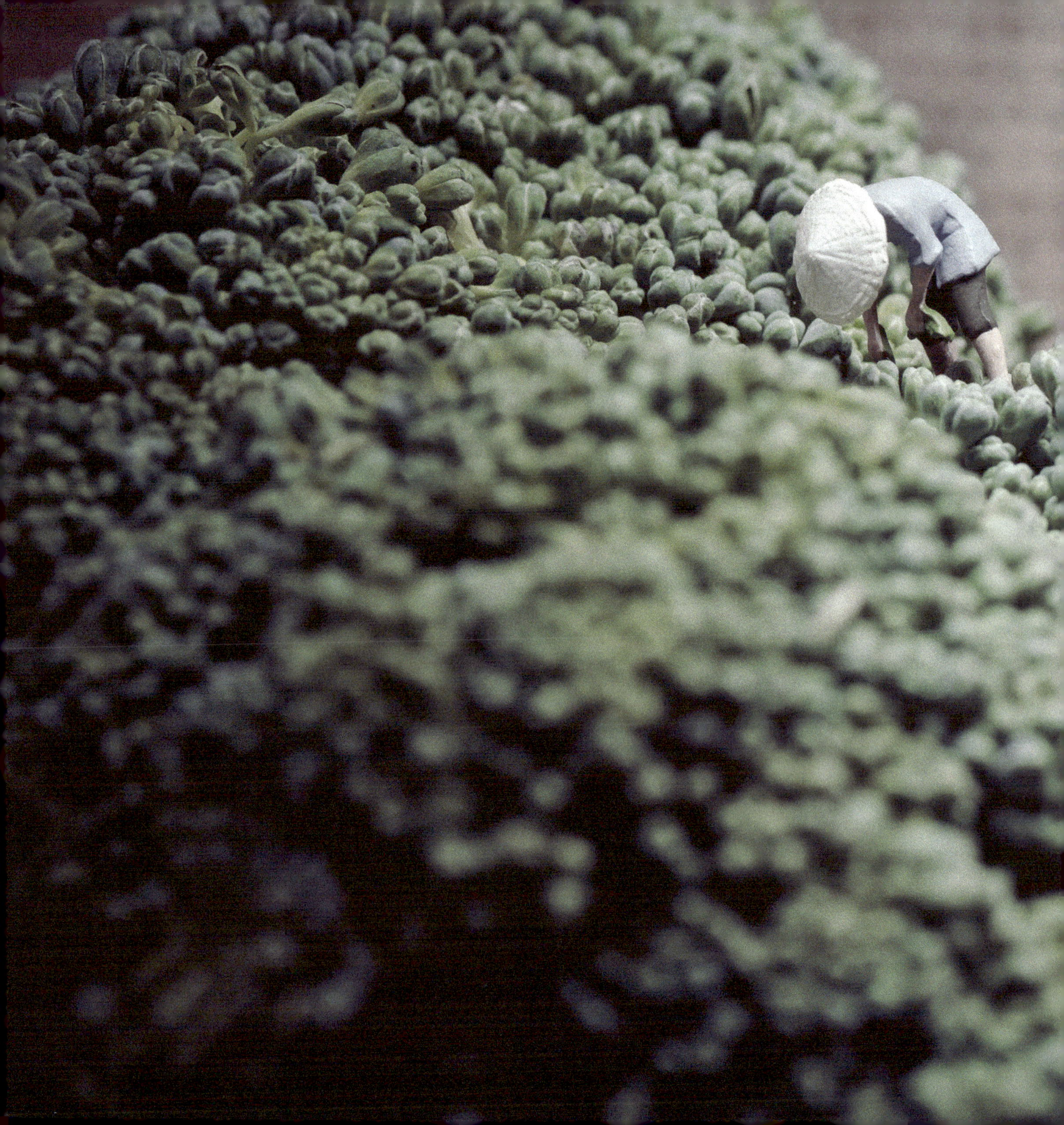

The Farmers/Peasants

The Artisans

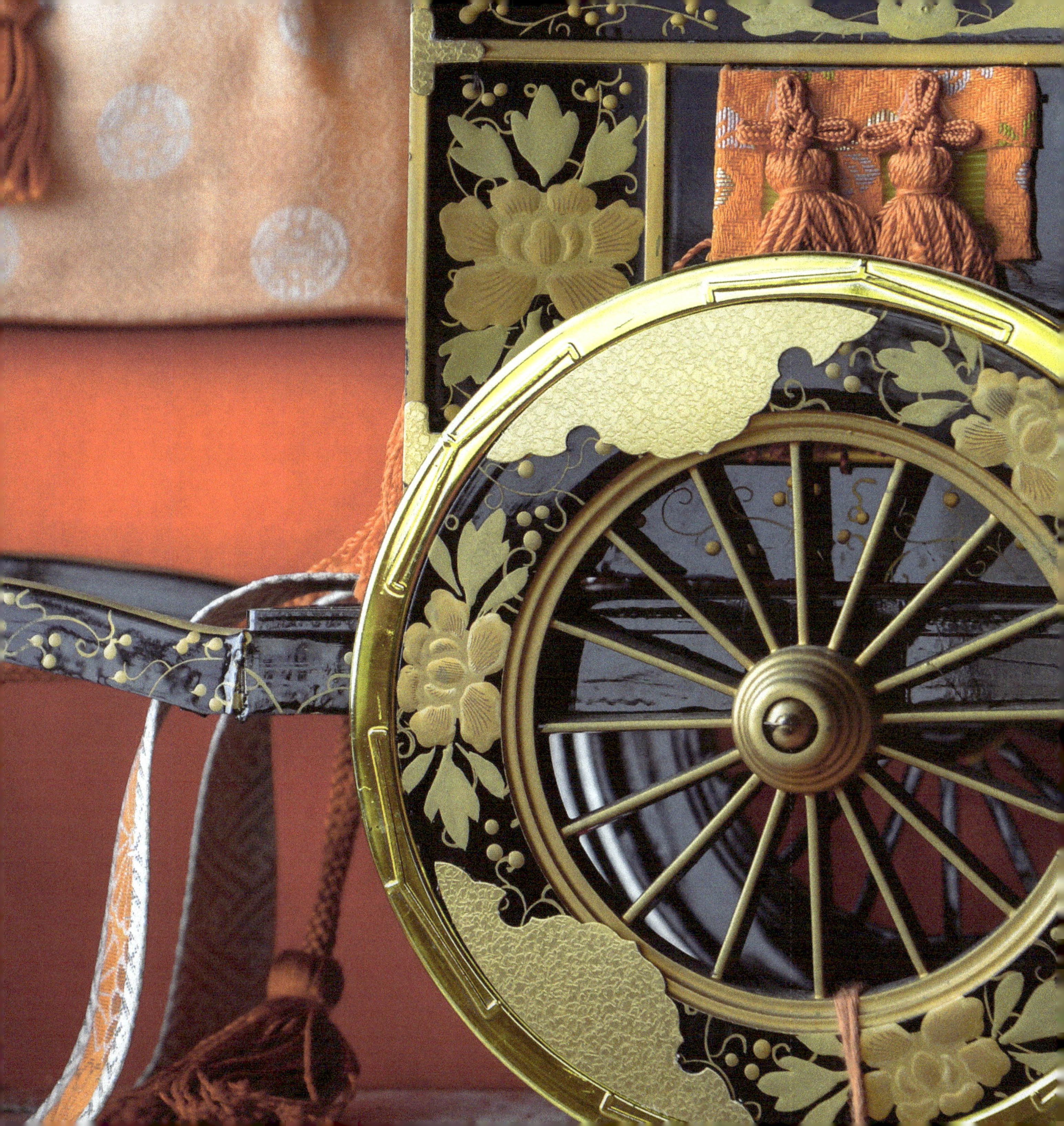

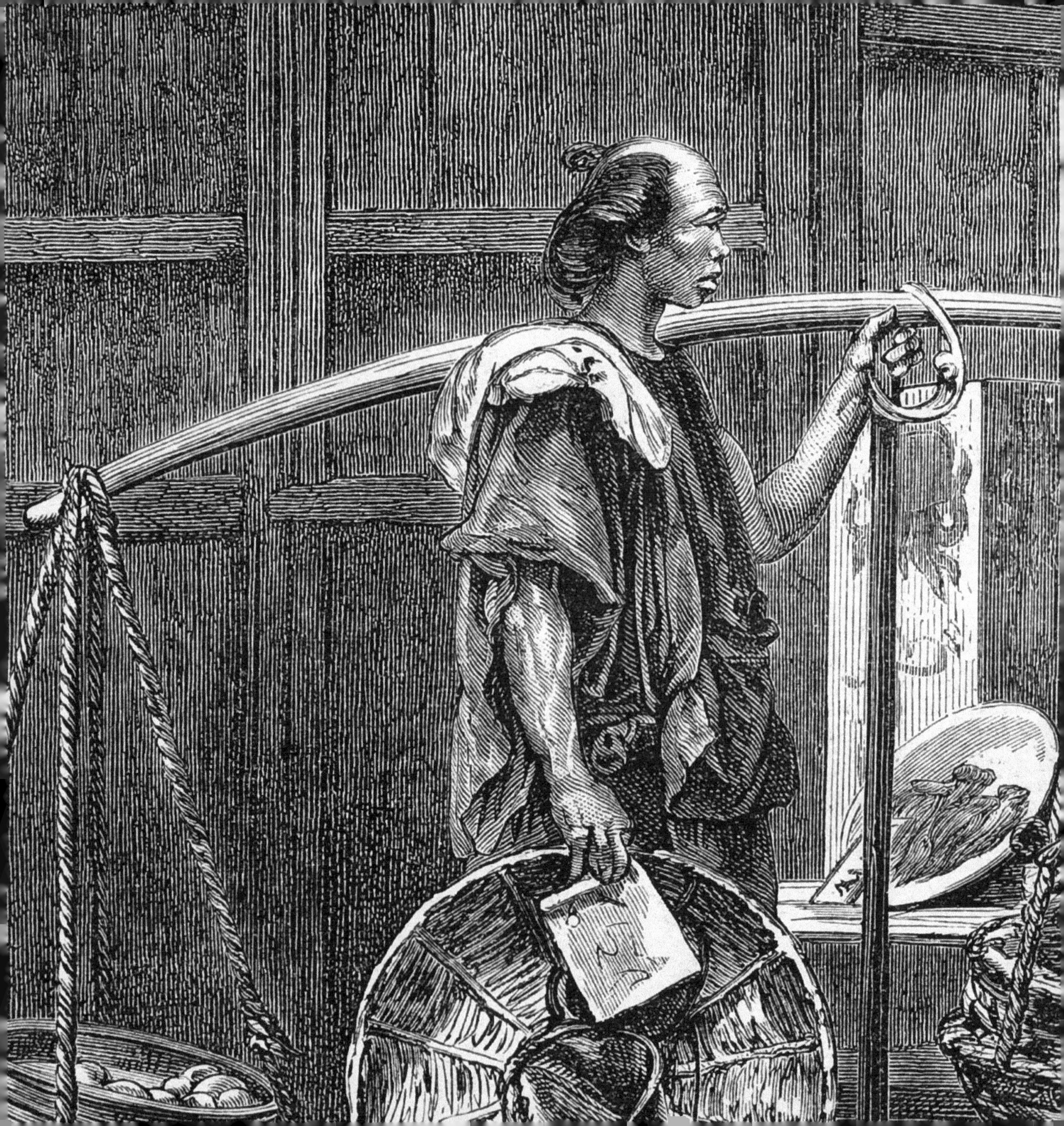

The Merchants

The **Japanese History** is very interesting, research and learn more!

PAN

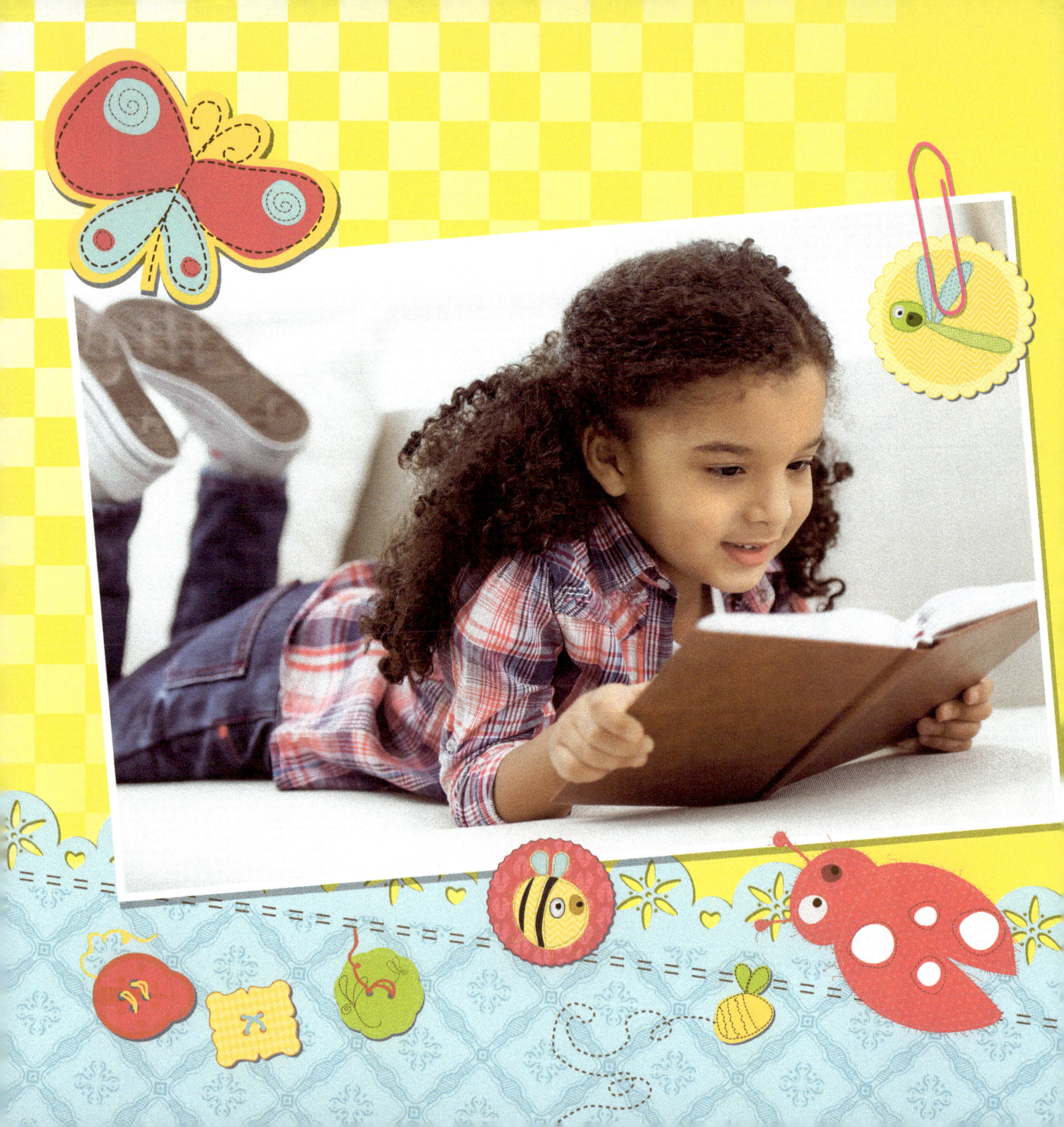

Visit

BABY PROFESSOR
EDUCATION KIDS

www.BabyProfessorBooks.com

to download Free Baby Professor eBooks and view our catalog of new and exciting Children's Books

Milton Keynes UK
Ingram Content Group UK Ltd.
UKHW050735160224
437882UK00007B/11